# Being Mindful

Katie Peters

GRL Consultants,
Diane Craig and Monica Marx,
Certified Literacy Specialists

Pull Ahead Readers
People Smarts

Lerner Publications ◆ Minneapolis

**Note from a GRL Consultant**
This Pull Ahead leveled book has been carefully designed for beginning readers. A team of guided reading literacy experts has reviewed and leveled the book to ensure readers pull ahead and experience success.



Lerner Publications Company
An imprint of Lerner Publishing Group, Inc.
241 First Avenue North
Minneapolis, MN 55401 USA

For reading levels and more information, look up this title at www.lernerbooks.com.

Main body text set in Memphis Pro 24/39
Typeface provided by Linotype.

Photo Acknowledgments
The images in this book are used with the permission of: © FG Trade/Getty Images, pp. 10–11; © galitskaya/Getty Images, pp. 12–13, 16 (stretching); © Jasonfang/Getty Images, pp. 4–5, 16 (listening); © Morsa Images/Getty Images, pp. 14–15; © Ridofranz/Getty Images, pp. 8–9, 16 (hugging); © StockPlanets/Getty Images, pp. 6–7; © subodhsathe/Getty Images, p. 3.

Front cover: © Monika Gniot/Shutterstock Images

**Library of Congress Cataloging-in-Publication Data**

Names: Peters, Katie, author.
Title: Being mindful / Katie Peters.
Description: Minneapolis : Lerner Publications, 2022. | Series: Helpful habits (pull ahead readers people smarts - nonfiction) | Includes index. | Audience: Ages 4–7 | Audience: Grades K–1 | Summary: "When children experience difficult feelings, show them how they can help themselves feel better by pausing and being mindful in the moment. Pairs with the fiction title Isaac's Tree"— Provided by publisher.
Identifiers: LCCN 2020015155 (print) | LCCN 2020015156 (ebook) | ISBN 9781728403472 (library binding) | ISBN 9781728423197 (paperback) | ISBN 9781728418353 (ebook)
Subjects: LCSH: Mindfulness (Psychology)—Juvenile literature. | Awareness—Juvenile literature.
Classification: LCC BF637.M56 P48 2021 (print) | LCC BF637.M56 (ebook) | DDC 155.4/1913—dc23

LC record available at https://lccn.loc.gov/2020015155
LC ebook record available at https://lccn.loc.gov/2020015156

Manufactured in the United States of America
1 - 48343 - 48885 - 1/25/2021

# Table of Contents

# Being Mindful

Sometimes I am sad.
I listen to music.
This helps me feel better.

Sometimes I am angry.
I take deep breaths.
This helps me feel better.

Sometimes I am scared.

I hug my bear.

This helps me feel better.

Sometimes I am worried.
I think about a happy place.
This helps me feel better.

Sometimes I am hurt.
I stretch my body.
This helps me feel better.

Sometimes I am happy.
It feels good to be happy.

Close your eyes and take a deep breath. How does this feel?

## Did You See It?

hugging

listening

stretching

## Index